"Saint Augustine once counseled that the top three virtues of Christianity are 'Humility, humility, and humility.' One suspects he said this because when humility is intact, all other fruit of the Spirit fall into place. What Gavin Ortlund has given us in this wonderful book is not only a description of humility but also a pathway that makes the reader desire more of it, for the smaller we become in our own eyes, the bigger Christ becomes to us. I can't recommend this book highly enough."

Scott Sauls, Senior Pastor, Christ Presbyterian Church, Nashville, Tennessee; author, *Beautiful People Don't Just Happen*

"If humble people are realists (and they are), and if realists are humble people (and they are), then Ortlund's concise work helpfully jabs us awake from our dreamy delusions of self-identity (whether too inflated or too deflated) and gives us very practical help in constructing our lives according to the plumb line of Christlike realism. Wisely, Ortlund wants us to not only understand humility but pursue it, experience it, feel it, and even enjoy it. Making reference to gems by Churchill, Lewis, Keller, Wesley, Edwards, Aquinas, Kidner, ten Boom, Augustine, Spurgeon, and more, Ortlund guides us away from misconceptions and toward genuine love, even tackling the dreaded concept of submission. I'm glad I read it."

Sam Crabtree, Pastor for Small Groups, Bethlehem Baptist Church, Minneapolis, Minnesota; author, *Practicing Affirmation*

"In today's high-pressure world of Christian ministry, it is all too easy to adopt attitudes that are antithetical to those modeled by Christ. Pride is often considered a necessary component in the advancement of the kingdom, and humility is viewed as a weakness that is to be overcome. In this insightful book, Gavin Ortlund reminds us that humility is the way of Jesus and the only real option for his servants. A much-needed word in our time."

Brian Brodersen, Pastor, Calvary Chapel Costa Mesa, Santa Ana, California

"There are timely books and there are timeless ones; fortunately, Gavin Ortlund's new book, *Humility*, happens to be both. In a culture of bravado and hubris, Gavin shows us the beauty and freedom of humility—not mere kindness, sweetness, and a nonoffensive personality, but humility as the redemptive DNA of the gospel, the heartbeat of Jesus's incarnation, and the culture God's Spirit creates in a heart and church alive to the riches of grace. What a compelling, inviting, life-giving study."

Scotty Smith, Pastor Emeritus, Christ Community Church, Franklin, Tennessee; Teacher in Residence, West End Community Church, Nashville, Tennessee

"In an age of self-creation and self-promotion, this book serves as a reset. The burden of creating one's own image and work is heavy. We feel a compulsion to prove our worth and tell others about it. But Gavin reminds us that it's self-forgetfulness, not self-promotion, that leads us to joy. He puts on display the relief of humility and the comfort that comes with personally knowing the goodness and compassion of God. In an age where we feel the pressure to put ourselves front and center, this book is a needed correction and a sweet exhortation to instead hide ourselves in Jesus."

Jen Oshman, author, *Enough about Me* and *Cultural Counterfeits*

Humility

Growing Gospel Integrity

Michael Reeves, series editor

Humility: The Joy of Self-Forgetfulness, Gavin Ortlund

Humility

The Joy of Self-Forgetfulness

Gavin Ortlund

CROSSWAY®

WHEATON, ILLINOIS

Humility: The Joy of Self-Forgetfulness

Copyright © 2023 by Gavin Ortlund

Published by Crossway
               1300 Crescent Street
               Wheaton, Illinois 60187

Published in association with the literary agency of Wolgemuth & Associates.

Cover design: Jordan Singer

First printing, 2023

Printed in the United States of America

Trade paperback ISBN: 978-1-4335-8230-1
ePub ISBN: 978-1-4335-8233-2
PDF ISBN: 978-1-4335-8231-8
Mobipocket ISBN: 978-1-4335-8232-5

Library of Congress Control Number: 2022944938

Crossway is a publishing ministry of Good News Publishers.

VP			31	30	29	28	27	26	25	24	23
14	13	12	11	10	9	8	7	6	5	4	3	2	1

In memory of my grandfather,
Ray Ortlund Sr.,
who modeled through his life that humility
leads to contagious joyfulness

Contents

Series Preface

GOSPEL INTEGRITY IS, I suggest, the greatest and most vital need of the church today. More than moral behavior and orthodox beliefs, this integrity that we need is a complete alignment of our heads, our hearts, and our lives with the truths of the gospel.

In his letter to the Philippians, the apostle Paul issues a call to his readers to live as people of the gospel. Spelling out what this means, Paul sets out four marks of gospel integrity.

First, he entreats, "Let your manner of life be worthy of the gospel of Christ" (1:27a). The people of the gospel should live lives *worthy* of the gospel.

Second, this means "standing firm in one spirit, with one mind striving side by side for the faith of the gospel" (1:27b). In other words, integrity to the gospel requires a *united* stand of faithfulness together.

Third, knowing that such a stand will mean suffering and conflict (1:29–30), Paul calls the Philippians not to be "frightened in anything" (1:28a). He describes this *courage* as "a clear sign" of our salvation (1:28b).

Fourth, Paul writes,

> So if there is any encouragement in Christ, any comfort from love, any participation in the Spirit, any affection and sympathy, complete my joy by being of the same mind, having the same love, being in full accord and of one mind. Do nothing from selfish ambition or conceit, but in humility count others more significant than yourselves. (2:1–3)

Paul thus makes it clear that there is no true Christian integrity without *humility*.

The simple aim of this series is to reissue Paul's gospel-based call to an integrity that means living *worthily*, *unitedly*, *courageously*, and *humbly*. We need to recognize, however, that these four marks are not abstract moral qualities or virtues. What Paul has in mind are, quite specifically, marks and manifestations *of integrity to the gospel*. As such, the books in this series will unpack how the gospel fuels and shapes those qualities in us.

Through this little series, may God be glorified, and may "the grace of the Lord Jesus Christ be with your spirit" (4:23).

Michael Reeves
Series Editor

Preface

SOMEONE INNOCENTLY ASKED what it's like to write a book about humility. I thought of Winston Churchill's reputed quip about a political opponent: "He is a humble man, but then, he has much to be humble about!"[1]

This is my only qualification for writing this book: I have much to be humble about!

But humility is too wonderful a thing for us not to consider and pursue. It is like oxygen. Humility is restorative, normalizing. It is for your soul what a good night's sleep is for your body.

As we start together in this book, here's an image to help orient us. Take a moment to think about what it feels like to

---

1   This quotation has appeared in various forms. One appeared in William Henry Chamberlin, "The So Austere, So Safe Clement Attlee," *Chicago Tribune*, June 27, 1954.

be truly *awed* by something. For instance, consider the feeling you have when you stare up at the immensity of a night sky full of stars and become overwhelmed with how small you are and how huge the universe is. Think of the particular nuances of this feeling—the sense of wonder, of enchantment, of losing track of yourself. It is one of the most wonderful feelings you will ever have.

Humility is the pathway to that feeling. Humility can lead you to that feeling continuously, in all kinds of scenes.

After all, the world is chock-full of things that should inspire our awe. Cloud formations. The movements of ants. Mathematical equations. Trees that have been alive since before the time of Christ. The way a baby grows in the womb. The story of the person who works in the cubicle next to you. There are no uninteresting objects, only uninterested subjects. There is no reason not to live with a kind of astonished gratitude at what is around us—except a lack of humility.

Humility opens our eyes to the wonders all around us: it is sensitivity to reality, the turning of our narrow selves to the vast ocean of externality, and ultimately to God himself. In this way, humility is, in every circumstance, the key to joy, flourishing, and life itself.

This book was written to help us understand and pursue humility. It was written especially for Christians, and chapter 4 has an eye to pastors and church leaders—but I hope anyone might benefit from it. The first half of the book considers personal humility, while the second half considers humility in the context of the church. Throughout, the goal is to understand one particular quality of humility: namely, its ability to lead us back to joy.

Special thanks to Justin Taylor and the entire team at Crossway for being a joy for an author to work with—they are professional, courteous, generous, and so skilled at what they do. Greg Bailey's sharp editorial comments improved the book in many ways. I'm grateful to Mike Reeves for his gracious invitation to be a part of this fantastic series. Thanks also to Andrew Wolgemuth for his help, encouragement, and friendship in my writing. And most of all, thank you, Esther, for being such a friend through the last several years. You alone understand. Psalm 27:13–14. Don't stop believing.

Introduction

Why We Misunderstand Humility

WE OFTEN THINK OF HUMILITY as a somewhat dreary virtue. We know we need it, but we don't expect it to be much fun.[1]

I remember hearing a talk on humility at a youth group. The speaker opened with dutiful reluctance: "I know we don't really enjoy this topic, but we need to talk about it anyway."

This is how many of us think: humility is important, but strictly as a duty. It's like paying our taxes or going to the dentist.

Interestingly, C. S. Lewis argued the opposite: "To get even near [humility], even for a moment, is like a drink of cold

---

1 Portions of this introduction are adapted from my article "Humility Isn't Hating Yourself: The Joy of Self-Forgetfulness," Desiring God, August 19, 2019, https://www.desiringgod.org/articles/.

water to a man in a desert."[2] Tim Keller preached something similar: "There's nothing more relaxing than humility."[3] As he explained, pride grumbles at everything, but humility can joyfully receive life as a gift.

So perhaps we get it backward: we think humility is an impossible burden, but in reality it is as light as a feather. It is pride that makes life gray and drab; humility brings out the color.

Misconceptions about Humility

Why do we get this wrong? I don't fully know, but I suspect that part of the answer is that we simply misunderstand what humility is. It may be the most misunderstood virtue there is. Here are three misconceptions, in particular.

Misconception #1: Humility Is Hiding

Humility is *not* hiding your talents or abilities. If you can paint like Van Gogh, humility does not require you to keep your work under a veil in the basement closet. If you can

---

2 C. S. Lewis, *Mere Christianity*, in *The Complete C. S. Lewis Signature Classics* (San Francisco: HarperSanFrancisco, 2002), 71–72.

3 Cited in Bethany Jenkins, "There's Nothing More Relaxing Than Humility," The Gospel Coalition, November 5, 2015, https://www.thegospelcoalition.org/.

pitch a ninety-five-mile-per-hour fastball, humility will not encourage you to sit on the bench and never tell the coach.

In Lewis's classic *The Screwtape Letters*, one devil advises another,

> The Enemy [God] wants to bring the man to a state of mind in which he could design the best cathedral in the world, and know it to be the best, and rejoice in the fact, without being any more (or less) or otherwise glad at having done it than he would be if it had been done by another. The Enemy wants him, in the end, to be so free from any bias in his own favor that he can rejoice in his own talents as frankly and gratefully as in his neighbor's talents—or in a sunrise, an elephant, or a waterfall.[4]

If Lewis is right, then denying your talents is not humility—if anything, it is the opposite, since you are still focused on yourself, biased for or against yourself as an exception to the rest of the human race. Humility means the death of this

---

4 C. S. Lewis, *The Screwtape Letters*, in *The Complete C. S. Lewis Signature Classics*, 153–54.

craving, self-referential framework. It means the freedom of valuing your contribution to the world alongside every other good thing in the world.

Imagine it like this: you are part of a team of doctors working to cure a disease. You make a discovery that contributes approximately 25 percent toward finding the cure. Another doctor then makes a different discovery that contributes the remaining 75 percent toward finding the cure. Humility means you are pleased with your accomplishment and able to speak freely about it, while simultaneously and effortlessly three times more pleased with your colleague's effort.

To be such a person is not a burden, but joy and freedom.

Misconception #2: Humility Is Self-Hatred

Humility is *not* self-hatred, self-neglect, or self-punishment. The Bible never says, "Hate yourself; instead, love your neighbor." It says, "Love your neighbor as yourself" (Lev. 19:18). Self-hatred is actually no less sinful than hatred of others (just as suicide is a form of murder).

Musician Andrew Peterson has a song entitled "Be Kind to Yourself." It's quite a lovely song. But this idea of self-kindness strikes some of us as strange—and, to be sure, it can be misunderstood. It must be distinguished from self-indulgence, for instance. But there is a way to take care of yourself, to genuinely have regard for yourself, that is healthy and good, and ultimately makes you more useful to others. As I often say in counseling situations, self-care is not selfish.

Many in our society struggle with a sense of shame, inferiority, and low self-worth. We must sharply distinguish such feelings from the goal of humility. Whatever else humility will require of you, it will never rob you of your dignity as an image bearer of God.

Humble people don't need constant attention, but they also don't necessarily *mind* being noticed. Humble people don't need flattery, but they can sincerely receive a compliment. Such people are not constantly minimizing themselves. They can walk into a room with a bounce in their step, open to what their presence might contribute to others (but not needing it to).

Again, to be such a person is not a burden, but joy and freedom.

Misconception #3: Humility Is Weakness

Humility is *not* weakness. We often think of it this way—as though humble people are the type you can push around if you want. They think so lowly of themselves that they don't stand up against opposition.

But the truth is once again close to the opposite. Humility actually breeds strength and resilience because it frees us from the restricting needs of the ego—the need to be in charge, the need to look good, the need to defend ourselves, and so on. Humble people are often marked by a healthy ability to speak their minds on a given subject. They are not distracted by the burdens of constant self-regard and self-assessment.

Humility also breeds strength because it is motivating. There is nothing like freedom from self-awareness and self-protectiveness that so wonderfully concentrates you on the matter in front of you. As a result, humble people tend to be productive and industrious, often without even thinking about it.

So again, humility is not a burden but a joy. It feels like discovering how something is supposed to work (that "something" being yourself).

Humility Is Self-Forgetfulness Leading to Joy

Okay, this gives us a sense of what humility isn't—but what is it, exactly?

Keller, following Lewis, speaks of humility as self-forgetfulness—it's not thinking less of yourself, but thinking of yourself less.[5] Self-hiding, self-hatred, self-protection—

---

5   Timothy Keller, *The Freedom of Self-Forgetfulness: The Path to True Christian Joy* (Leyland, England, UK: 10Publishing, 2012).

these are all forms of self-preoccupation, whereas humility leads us into freedom from thoughts of self altogether.

Lewis helps us once again:

> Do not imagine that if you meet a really humble man he will be what most people call "humble" nowadays: he will not be a sort of greasy, smarmy person, who is always telling you that, of course, he is nobody. Probably all you will think about him is that he seemed a cheerful, intelligent chap who took a real interest in what you said to him. If you do dislike him it will be because you feel a little envious of anyone who seems to enjoy life so easily. He will not be thinking about humility: he will not be thinking about himself at all.[6]

The word *cheerful* strikes me in this passage, as well as the emphasis on the enjoyment of life. This is the particular theme we will explore in this book: the pleasantness of humility. When we see humility in others, it is attractive, charming, and winsome. When we practice it ourselves, life goes more smoothly and happily.

In fact, we can go so far as to identify joy as the acid test of humility, for true humility always produces joy. If we lack

6   Lewis, *Mere Christianity*, in *The Complete C. S. Lewis Signature Classics*, 72.

joy, we know we've got a counterfeit humility. Something is misfiring. Of course, this doesn't mean that humility will always feel uplifting and comfortable. There will be arduous moments. But the net result will be, as with exercise or a healthy diet, distinctly pleasant.

So we can think of humility like this: self-forgetfulness leading to joy.

We will develop this throughout the rest of the book, but as an entry point, consider this wonderful passage from J. R. R. Tolkien's story *The Hobbit*. It's the conclusion of the book, after the Hobbit Bilbo Baggins has returned home and is reflecting on his adventures with his friend, the wizard Gandalf.

"Then the prophecies of the old songs have turned out to be true, after a fashion!" said Bilbo.

"Of course!" said Gandalf. "And why should not they prove true? Surely you don't disbelieve the prophecies, because you had a hand in bringing them about yourself? You don't really suppose, do you, that all your adventures and escapes were managed by mere luck, just for your sole benefit? You are a very fine person, Mr. Baggins, and I am very fond of you; but you are only quite a little fellow in a wide world after all!"

"Thank goodness!" said Bilbo laughing, and handed him the tobacco-jar.[7]

Oh, how I love this passage. It conveys a sense of the *relief* of humility. Being a big deal is a burden. Humility, in contrast, means you don't interpret everything in relation to yourself, and you don't need to. It is the death of the narrow, suffocating filter of self-referentiality. It is the nourishing, calming acceptance that you have a small place in a much larger story: that your life is being guided by something far bigger than your plans or controls, and serving something far bigger than your "sole benefit."

Humility is the joy of embracing life as it is meant to be lived. Humility is accepting Gandalf's rebuke that "you are only quite a little fellow in a wide world after all" and responding, like Bilbo, with relief and laughter.

We are tiny people in a vast world: thank goodness!

Discussion Questions

1. What do you think is the biggest misconception about humility today?

---

7 J. R. R. Tolkien, *The Hobbit* (New York: Houghton Mifflin, 1982), 305.

2. Have you ever seen—in yourself or others—humility confused with self-hatred? What was the result of that error?

3. Do you agree or disagree that joy is the acid test of humility? Why or why not?

PART 1

Cultivating Personal Humility

How the Gospel Defines Humility

IF YOU HEAR SOMEONE DESCRIBED as "a really humble person," what comes to mind?

Often we think of how humility plays out, first and foremost, toward other people. Humble people are not "one-uppers," for example. They apologize more, they notice others more, and so forth.

There is much truth to this, but we should first conceptualize humility in relation to God. All true humility starts before God himself, then trickles out into our other relationships. And, in the other direction (here is a sobering thought!): all pride, before it is ever directed to other people, is first directed to God.

One of the great themes of the Bible is the importance of humility before God: "God opposes the proud but gives grace to the humble" (James 4:6). God himself declares that the one he regards is "humble and contrite in spirit and trembles at my word" (Isa. 66:2).

But what does it mean, exactly, to be humble before God? How does God define humility?

In order to answer this question, we must begin with what God himself has done for us in the gospel. God has not merely given us an abstract definition of humility—in the person of Jesus Christ, he has himself (astonishingly!) *displayed* humility.

The Incarnation Is the Supreme Act of Humility

The central belief of Christian theology is what we call the incarnation—the belief that God became man. It is a staggering idea on many levels, but most breathtaking of all, perhaps, is what it reveals of divine humility.

Can we even speak of *divine humility*? Dare we think that God himself is humble? Or is humility only proper to creatures?

This is a complicated question, and we won't get into all the nuances here.[1] But this much is certain: we can indeed conceive of Christ's incarnation as an expression of humil-

---

1 For a defense of divine humility, see Matthew A. Wilcoxen, *Divine Humility: God's Morally Perfect Being* (Waco, TX: Baylor University Press, 2019).

ity. This is how the apostle Paul speaks in his letter to the Philippians:

> Have this mind among yourselves, which is yours in Christ Jesus, who, though he was in the form of God, did not count equality with God a thing to be grasped, but emptied himself, by taking the form of a servant, being born in the likeness of men. And being found in human form, *he humbled himself* by becoming obedient to the point of death, even death on a cross. (2:5–8)

Why is the incarnation an act of humility? First, Paul speaks of it as a kind of *emptying*: Christ did not cling to his divine rights, but emptied himself by becoming a man. It is important to clarify that this does not mean that Christ in any way ceased to be God (it has sometimes been misunderstood that way). Nonetheless, the act of taking on a human nature can be spoken of as a kind of emptying: a lowering, a condescension, a descent.

Second, Paul characterizes the incarnation as an expression of *servanthood*. By becoming man, Christ took "the form of a servant." The climactic moment of this act of servanthood was when Christ humbled himself by accepting death by crucifixion, followed by his burial in a borrowed tomb.

It's not hard to see how God becoming man can be described as an act of humility. In fact, no act could ever possibly be a greater demonstration of humility. You might think you've seen people display humility before—for instance, when an important adult gets down on the floor to play with a little child. But could there be any greater descent than for God to become a human baby? For the Creator to lie dead in a tomb?

Let's just pause and dwell on this mind-boggling thought for a moment: *God became a baby.* The transcendent Son of God, adored by angels, through whom every star was made, while remaining fully God, lowered himself to the status of a fetus growing in Mary's womb. Can you fathom it?[2]

Theologians often describe the period of Christ's incarnate work leading up to his death and burial as his "state of humiliation." This is in contrast to his "state of exaltation," consisting of his resurrection, ascension, and heavenly rule. For example, the Westminster Shorter Catechism uses the label *humiliation* to describe Christ's "being born, and that in a low condition, made under the law, undergoing the miseries of this life, the wrath of God, and the cursed death of the

2 I wrestled with some of the ideas that follow on my personal blog in "What Amazed Me This Year about Christmas," Truth Unites, December 13, 2014, https://gavinortlund.com/.

cross; in being buried, and continuing under the power of death for a time."[3]

Consider this word *humiliation* for a moment. Have you ever been humiliated? Do you remember that feeling? This is the word, albeit with some distinct nuance, that theologians use to describe *what God himself did*.

God, the Lord himself, the Almighty, humbled himself— *to the point of crucifixion*—for us and for our sins.

Lord, we marvel at your stunning display of humility. You, the Most High, have not refrained from taking the lowest and worst position imaginable. O Lord, how foolish all our pride seems when we remember the cross! Help us to follow your example, Lord. Teach us the pathway of humility.

The Details of the Incarnation Reflect Humility

We can go even further. As if it was not enough for God to become man, when he did so, it was in humble circumstances. He not only stooped down to the lowest place, but he did so—if I may put it like this—quietly, unassumingly.

I first began to reflect on this a few years ago during the Christmas season. Each year during advent, we often hear

---

3   The Westminster Shorter Catechism, Question 27, in *The Westminster Confession of Faith* (Glasgow: Free Presbyterian, 1966), 294.

the same Scripture passages read over and over, reminding us of the wonderful Christmas story. During one service, it suddenly occurred to me to wonder about the story of the angels' appearance to the shepherds (Luke 2:8–20).

The thought came: Why involve these shepherds at all? We've already got several other angelic visits (Matt. 1:20; 2:13, 19) and seemingly more important characters responding to the events, such as the wise men (2:1–12). Why send a whole multitude of angels out to the rural fields for only a few shepherds to notice? Why not spread the news further?

The more I considered this, the more I began to notice how all kinds of other details in the Christmas story reflect a kind of quiet humility. For example:

- Jesus could have beamed down as a full-grown man; instead, he was born as a baby.
- He could have at least been born in a palace; instead, he was laid in a manger where animals fed.
- He could have been rich or a prince; instead, he was born into poverty to become a carpenter.
- He could have been born in a city (such as Rome, or at least Jerusalem); instead, he was born in rural Bethlehem.

Just consider it! The most important moment in history, the event that triggered the redemption of the whole world, the union of Creator and creation—and almost nobody knew. God limited the revelation of angelic rejoicing to a few rural shepherds, while all the important people of the world went about their business. "The world was made through him, yet the world did not know him" (John 1:10).

Now bear in mind, the one who was sleeping in the manger was the same one who "upholds the universe by the word of his power" (Heb. 1:3); even while he nursed at Mary's breast, it remained true that "in him all things hold together" (Col. 1:17). He was baby and Lord all at once. The juxtapositions of the Christmas story are mind-boggling:

- filling the heavens, yet swaddled tightly
- holding every atom in place, yet clinging to his mother
- sustaining the fiery stars, yet crying and needing Mary's comfort
- adored by the angels, yet sleeping amongst the donkeys

Again, you might think that when God did this, it would at least have made the headlines! This was the most significant turning point in the history of created reality. Yet there was no parade. No fanfare. The angels sang their herald to . . . a few rural shepherds.

When I contemplate the unpretentiousness of the gospel, I am ashamed of times I try to be noticed. Who am I to draw attention to myself when *God himself* took the hidden road?

O Lord, when we consider what you have done for us, we are ashamed of our fragile egos. We feel like the great hymn puts it: "My richest gain I count but loss, and pour contempt on all my pride." Help us follow your example of humility. Help us to pour contempt on all our pride.

Who Can Be Arrogant When Standing beside the Cross?

D. A. Carson tells the story of interviewing two famous theologians and asking them how they stayed humble despite all their accomplishments. One of them, in a kind of "gentle outrage," responded by asking, "How on earth can anyone be arrogant when standing beside the cross?"[4]

Indeed. Who of us can possibly be arrogant while remembering Bethlehem and Golgotha? If God himself has taken the lowest position, who are we to seek importance?

4 D. A. Carson, *Basics for Believers: An Exposition of Philippians* (Grand Rapids, MI: Baker, 1996), 58.

The incarnation also compels us to ask: Who are the shepherds in the world today? What are the mangers in our lives? Where is the work of the cross happening now? This is God's pattern: he often shows up in a package that is all too easy to reject, to despise, to overlook. Humility is always God's way.

What are the unseen angels singing about right now? Be assured it is little noted by the world. It will sneak undetected under the radar of human pride, just as God himself did when he came into our world.

O God, you are the God of mangers, not palaces. Open our eyes to see you at work all around us.

Discussion Questions

1. Is it correct to say that God is humble? Are there any dangers in how such a statement might be understood?

2. What do you think it means to say that Christ "emptied himself" (Phil. 2:7)?

3. Which detail of the Christmas story stands out to you most as an expression of divine humility?

2

How the Gospel
Fuels Humility

THE LAST CHAPTER DESCRIBED how God has shown humility to us in the gospel. This chapter describes the reverse: how we are to respond to the gospel with humility.

This is how it must work: our pursuit of humility must start with what Christ has done for us in his incarnation and death. The gospel teaches us that through the work of Christ we can be fully forgiven and restored to our Creator God as we turn away from our sins and surrender our lives to Christ.

The gospel, then, is the source of all true humility. Humility is not a virtue we cultivate in the abstract; it is a mark of integrity to the gospel, and all our efforts at humility must be fueled by the gospel lest they result in mere fleshly counterfeits or imitations.

Is Pursuing Humility Inherently Prideful?

This reference to "fleshly counterfeits" brings up an objection that we should address up front, and some of you might already have worried about it: Should we be deliberate about cultivating humility? If humility is self-forgetfulness, isn't there a danger that working hard at it could become counterproductive? Indeed, couldn't it even lead *toward* fleshly counterfeits, as distinct from a gospel-fueled humility?

This is a valid danger. I have often heard Tim Keller say, "Humility is so shy. If you begin talking about it, it leaves." As C. S. Lewis noted, we can even take pride in our own humility! In *The Screwtape Letters*, one devil counsels another,

> Your patient has become humble; have you drawn his attention to the fact? All virtues are less formidable to us once the man is aware that he has them, but this is specially true of humility. Catch him at the moment when he is really poor in spirit and smuggle into his mind the gratifying reflection, "By jove! I'm being

humble," and almost immediately pride—pride at his own humility—will appear.[1]

At every step along the way, we must be alert to this danger of false humility. However, I don't believe this means that we should never think about and intentionally pursue humility (though it is certainly a good reason not to take ourselves too seriously in the process!).

For one thing, deliberate reflection about humility is a historic Christian practice. The Bible is emphatic in calling us to practice humility. For instance, Philippians 2:5–11, the famous hymn we considered in the last chapter, serves as the rationale for Paul's preceding exhortation: "In humility count others more significant than yourselves" (2:3). There are many other passages we could mention. How can we obey verses such as Philippians 2:3 if we don't reflect on what they mean? In addition, great theologians such as Augustine, Basil, Thomas Aquinas, John Calvin, and Jonathan Edwards wrote extensively about what humility is and how we are to acquire it.

One help along the way will be our rubric that true humility always leads to joy. This is a good safeguard, because we

---

1   C. S. Lewis, *The Screwtape Letters*, in *The Complete C. S. Lewis Signature Classics* (San Francisco: HarperSanFrancisco, 2002), 153.

can pretend to have other virtues more easily than we can pretend to have joy. If you are pursuing humility in order to be humble, there is more temptation for this inward turn to a joyless, manufactured, artificial humility. But so long as you are pursuing humility in order to arrive upon reality and truth—the solid world around you—you are on safer ground.

So in other words, the goal is neither (1) to try super-duper hard to be humble nor (2) to never think about humility at all. It's something a bit more nuanced than either of these.

I propose the best way forward is to explore a gospel-shaped humility. This will help us avoid the unhealthy extremes. Let's consider two ways, in particular, that the gospel fuels humility.

The Gospel Fuels Humility by Showing Us Our Sins

If the theme of this book is that humility leads to joy, we must be equally clear that it does not typically *start* in joy. In fact, the pathway toward humility begins with facing a bitter fact: *we are not humble*. Lewis once again puts it well: "If anyone would like to acquire humility, I can, I think, tell you the first step. The first step is to realize that one is proud. And a biggish step, too."[2]

2   C. S. Lewis, *Mere Christianity*, in *The Complete C. S. Lewis Signature Classics*, 72.

I like Lewis's word *biggish*. It is a biggish step to admit we are proud. It's extremely hard to do. We naturally want to evade or downplay our need for humility. "It's not *that* bad," we say to ourselves. (And we can always compare ourselves to others in order to feel better.)

The gospel cures us of this because it teaches us to measure our pride by the cross of Jesus Christ. The cross shows us the depth of God's love, but it also shows us the depth of our sinful need. It reveals what God was willing to do, but it also reveals what he *had* to do. Our pride is such that it put the Son of God on the cross.

Let's not rush past this too quickly. Let's dwell on this sobering truth for a moment: *our sins put Jesus on the cross.*

Let me put it even more personally, for myself, and invite you to consider the same: *my sins put Jesus on the cross.*

It's a disquieting thought, isn't it? We want to squirm around it somehow. But we must face it, squarely and without evasion, in order to understand our true condition. The pathway to humility starts here, at the supreme offense of the cross, where our pride is stripped of every last rag of self-defense.

Francis Schaeffer used to say that "Christian faith means bowing twice." We bow before God first as the source of being and second as the source of morality. In other words, we bow first before God because we are creatures and he is Creator; then we bow again because we are sinners and he is Judge and Savior.[3]

When you think about it, the first of these is fully sufficient to motivate us toward humility. Every breath we breathe is a gift from God. He is the fount and source of everything. We are infinitely vulnerable before him—infinitely dependent, infinitely receptive.

But as if that is not enough, we *also* stand before him as sinners. We are like traitors returning to the rightful king, asking to rejoin his side, apologizing for our treason. A reason to bow twice, indeed—and to bow low!

I find it helpful to seek to position myself *as low as I am able* under this reality, fully accepting what the gospel teaches me about my sin. The words of the great hymn "And Can It Be That I Should Gain" help me:

And can it be that I should gain
An int'rest in the Savior's blood?
Died He for me, who caused His pain?
For me, who Him to death pursued?

---

3 Francis Schaeffer, *The God Who Is There*, in *The Francis A. Schaeffer Trilogy: The Three Essential Books in One Volume* (Wheaton, IL: Crossway, 1990), 146.

Amazing love! How can it be
That Thou, my God, shouldst die for me?[4]

Do you feel the wonder of these words? Can you say, with Wesley, that Christ died "for me, who Him to death pursued?" Can you say, "*I* caused his pain"? Granted, we may not have been there at the time of Jesus's crucifixion. But it was our sins that put him on the cross. John Stott put this wonderfully in his masterful book about the cross: "Before we can begin to see the cross as something done *for* us (leading us to faith and worship), we have to see it as something done by us (leading us to repentance)."[5]

It is here, at the foot of the cross, that real humility begins. This is the eye of the needle through which the camel of human pride must shrink and squeeze (Matt. 19:24). This is where we must be unmade before we can be remade.

Don't turn away in offense! If you can receive this, there is joy on the other side!

O Lord, give us hearts that can embrace this first step! Help us to humble ourselves under the weight of our true condition, our true need. Help us to measure ourselves by the cross.

4 From the hymn "And Can It Be That I Should Gain" by Charles Wesley, 1738.
5 John R. W. Stott, *The Cross of Christ*, 20th anniversary ed. (Downers Grove, IL: InterVarsity Press, 2006), 63, emphasis original.

The Gospel Fuels Humility by Showing Us God's Love

But we cannot stop there. True, gospel-fueled humility does not result simply from seeing our sins. That is just the first, preparatory step.

In his sermon "A Christian Spirit Is an Humble Spirit," Edwards distinguished between *legal* humiliation and *evangelical* humiliation. The former of these springs, he argued, from seeing God's greatness; even demons can feel something of this. But the latter springs from seeing God's loveliness; only a regenerate saint can experience this. As he put it,

> A sense of the loveliness of God is peculiarly that discovery of God which makes humility. A sense or discovery of God's greatness without his loveliness will not do it. But it is a discovery of his loveliness that is the very discovery that affects the thing and makes the soul humble.[6]

Edwards pointed out that the demons have a sense of God's greatness, and even shudder at it (James 2:19)—but it does not result in humility. Similarly, human beings can live in

6   Jonathan Edwards, *Charity and Its Fruits: Living in the Light of God's Love*, ed. Kyle Strobel (Wheaton, IL: Crossway, 2012), 152.

dread of God without real humility. We can even bewail our sins without arriving upon humility.

True humility, gospel-fueled humility, results from more than mere conviction or need: it results from personally *receiving* the provision of Christ as the remedy for that need. Ultimately, humility is the result not of desperation but of comfort. It flows from a deep-seated, heartfelt awareness of the love of God.

In other words, *evangelical humiliation*, to use Edwards's term, must eventually reverse Stott's formula: yes, the cross was done by us, but it also was done for us. Yes, Jesus had to bear our sins, but he bore them gladly, out of love.

How do we know if we have experienced this? I love Edwards's word: *loveliness*. Is God lovely to you? This is more than God being glorious or even generally merciful. Do you have a personal sweetness in your heart to him? Do you know deep down inside that you, even you, are his treasure and delight?

Think of the way you feel toward a friend who has kept your secrets, someone who has been there for you when you needed it. Think of that feeling of shared intimacy, of loyalty, of trust. Such feelings are *personal*. This is how we can experience the love of God: it is for *us*, in all our particular needs. It touches us at the deepest and most personal level of our being.

But why should this feeling of being so tenderly loved produce humility? After all, we have said that humility flows from thinking less of ourselves, not more.

To be sure, there are ways we can speak about God's love that make it all about us. At the same time, most of us have probably had the experience of being truly humbled by an act of kindness. Have you ever received an extremely generous gift or an unexpected and sincere apology? In its own way, kindness is humbling—it exposes and undermines our pride. It softens us.

Think of an analogy: Suppose you are approaching an extremely powerful king. You walk into the royal court. Your footsteps echo on the marble. The ceiling is far above. Gold glitters around the room. You look up to his high throne. You wait for him to speak. How does this feel? Humbling, to be sure.

But now suppose the king gets off his throne and rushes to you. He has been greatly worried about you. He has, in fact, put his life in great danger in order to help you. He embraces you and cries with relief that you are safe. Then he leads you to a huge table and personally serves you breakfast.

How do you feel now? Does not the king's kindness humble you as well—in a different (deeper) way?

This is the humility the gospel should produce in us. The Most High God has stooped down to show us a love that we could never have deserved, a love that will endure for all eternity. God has been to each of us like the father of the prodigal son—running to embrace us, welcoming us despite our shame, sparing no cost to celebrate our arrival.

How could we ever boast again? How could we not be softened?

O God, how can we possibly thank you for all you have done for us in Christ? "Were the whole realm of nature mine, that were a present far too small." Amen. All we can do is fall on our faces before you, with love and thankfulness and praise.

Seeing Ourselves without Being Crushed

In Lewis's *That Hideous Strength*, the character Mark is profoundly humbled by the suffering he has been through. He is about to be reunited to his wife, but he is almost ashamed to see her because he is looking back over his life and realizing what a fool he has been. For the first time in his life, he starts to understand how other people regard him: "He saw himself as this new circle must see him—as one more little vulgarian . . . dull, inconspicuous, frightened, calculating, cold. He wondered vaguely why he was like that."[7]

---

7   C. S. Lewis, *That Hideous Strength: A Modern Fairy-Tale for Grown-Ups* (New York: Scribner, 2003), 358.

A bit later, on the final pages of the book, he approaches his wife. His anguish is growing and growing. He is finally realizing that all his marriage he has lacked what Lewis calls "the humility of a lover." Lewis writes,

> Inch by inch, all the lout and clown and clod-hopper in him was revealed to his own reluctant inspection; the coarse, male boor with horny hands and hobnailed shoes and beefsteak jaw, not rushing in—for that can be carried off—but blundering, sauntering, stumping in where great lovers, knights and poets, would have feared to tread. . . . How had he dared? And who that understood could forgive him? He knew now what he must look like in the eyes of her friends and equals. Seeing that picture, he grew hot to the forehead.[8]

All of us will have moments of painful self-discovery like this—moments when we realize, with exquisite self-reproach, "Oh, *that's* what I'm like! *That* is how I come across! Yikes!"

The gospel enables us to embrace those moments without being crushed. The gospel fuels humility first by exposing our

8 Lewis, *That Hideous Strength*, 379.

sins, but then by covering them. "Where sin increased, grace abounded all the more" (Rom. 5:20).

In your most foolish moment, you are tenderly loved by Christ. His love for you is greater than your shame or regret. In whatever place you feel the sting of "legal humiliation," in that poignant area of need—*you are loved.*

Lewis's book ends with Mark going in and being embraced by his wife.

Discussion Questions

1. Do you agree that it is appropriate to intentionally seek humility? How do we know when our efforts at humility are becoming too self-preoccupied?

2. Which do you find more humbling: what the cross reveals of our sin or what it reveals of God's love? Why?

3

Ten Practices to Kill Pride

THUS FAR, WE'VE SEEN the "big picture" of how the gospel both defines and fuels humility. Now it's time to get more specific and practical about how we go about cultivating humility in our lives. This chapter focuses more on cultivating humility in our personal lives; the rest of the book focuses on how humility plays out in our corporate life as the church.

So here are ten ideas. These are somewhat random, and some may be more useful to you than others, so take the list as a whole as "food for thought."

Work at Listening

Do you recall C. S. Lewis's description of a humble person that we considered earlier: *a cheerful, intelligent chap who took a real interest in what you said to him?*

Lewis pinpoints one of the particularly refreshing qualities of humble people that you will quickly notice when interacting with them: they take a real interest in what you are saying. They *listen*.

Have you ever been talking to someone who isn't really listening to you? This person misses all the nuances. He filters everything you say through his own categories and jumps in before you've arrived at your point. You may find it impossible to alter this person's perspective with any new information. This is a good window into how pride works: it tends toward the gradual tuning out of everything external to the self. Humility is just the opposite: it wonderfully sharpens your attention to the vividness of what is around you, including the perspectives and thoughts of other people.

So our pursuit of humility should be part and parcel of our pursuit of being better listeners. Here are some ways humility encourages us to listen carefully:

1. Humility actually *values* the input of the speaker. It is not simply waiting until he or she is done to talk again. It approaches conversation more like a dance than a lecture, and as an opportunity to show love.

2. Humility refrains from too quickly arriving at a judgment. It feels no need to interpret and categorize others' words immediately. It is not threatened by the tension of uncertainty,

learning, and growth. It is willing to patiently wrestle with new information. It heeds the wonderful counsel of James: "Let every person be *quick to hear, slow to speak*" (James 1:19).

3. Humility does not filter information through its own previous categories. It does not assume that one idea is identical to another just because it is similar. It can make fine distinctions and appreciate the little nuances of a speaker's perspective.

4. Humility considers someone's speech in relation to that person's presuppositions. It asks, "How does this make sense to him?" and genuinely seeks to understand a different perspective on its own terms. It moves toward the speaker and exerts energy in trying to understand her.

5. Humility is not controlling. It doesn't need to run every conversation. It gives the speaker unhurried, unthreatened space in which to operate. It may sit in silence in one moment; in another, it may ask probing questions to draw the speaker out.

Do you see how wonderful it is to talk to such a person? Don't we all want to be more like this?

Practice Gratitude

A few years ago, I began to practice intentional gratitude, and I could write another book on all the ways it has been an enriching practice in my life. But I want to make just one point here: practicing intentional gratitude draws your attention to the blessings in your life.

Most of us tend to see the glass as half-empty. Our attention is instinctively drawn to what we lack or what we wish was different about our lives. When we practice gratitude, the opposite happens: our attention is drawn to the blessings in our lives, especially those that we tend to take for granted.

Having the ability to look around your life and say, "How am I so blessed?" is a wonderful pathway to humility.

Imagine getting to have dinner with your ten favorite celebrities. You are all sitting around a large dining room table, and you get to listen to the conversation, ask them questions, and get to know their personalities and backgrounds. Think of the sense of privilege you would have at the opportunity. You might think, "*Who am I*, that I get to be here and talk to all these people?"

This is what humility can do for us in *every* circumstance. Why should celebrities be the only people we feel privileged to be around? Every person you interact with is an image bearer of God. Every room you enter is an amazing corner of this world that God has made. Every blade of grass and tree leaf you see is a miracle of God's design. There is *nothing not to be astonished at*, if you really think about it.

Imagine the joy of walking into every situation wondering, "Who am I, that I get to be here? How did I get to be so fortunate? What a blessing to be alive, to be *here*, in *this* moment."

The deliberate cultivation of gratitude like this helps us approach all of life with humility, and it is almost impossible for such feelings not to produce joy.

Learn from Criticism

When you receive criticism, make it your practice to assume there is probably something to learn from it.

Our instinctive habit tends to be to stiff-arm and reject criticism because it hurts. And, to be sure, there are some forms of criticism we should simply ignore, especially criticism that is hateful, dishonest, or demeaning.

But most criticism we can learn from. Even if the critic is mostly wrong, there is usually *something* you can get from it.

The Bible has an enormous amount to say about listening to instruction and feedback. This is one of the great themes in the book of Proverbs, for example:

- "The way of a fool is right in his own eyes, but a wise man *listens* to advice" (Prov. 12:15).
- "A wise son hears his father's instruction, but a scoffer does not *listen* to rebuke" (Prov. 13:1).

- "Whoever ignores instruction despises himself, but he who *listens* to reproof gains intelligence" (Prov. 15:32).

Proud people often repeat mistakes because they do not learn from them. They tend to be impervious to feedback, brittle, and inflexible. They plow ahead regardless of consequences.

Humble people, by contrast, make continual course corrections based on the input of others. For humble people, 1 Corinthians 13:12 ("now we see in a mirror dimly") is not theoretical. They accept their limitations as an actuality and genuinely feel the need to incorporate the perspectives and insights of others.

This is why the word *teachableness* is nearly a synonym of *humility*. If you are looking for a basic indicator of humility, a good test is whether the person is teachable.

When someone criticizes you or you overhear some negative gossip about you, amid whatever else you need to do, can you take the time and vulnerability to ask, "What can I learn from this?" Over the long haul, this practice will be incredibly fruitful. Eventually it can become a habit. Just think of all you will have learned by the end of your life!

Cultivate the Enjoyment of Life

Humility can fully embrace the proper enjoyment of food, sleep, sex, vacation, throwing a Frisbee, enjoying a walk in the rain, or laughing at a hilarious joke. A humble person can receive it all, bit by bit, as a gift from God.

It might seem odd to speak of physical pleasures such as food or sex in a book on humility. Of course, it is true that these things can be abused, and I am thinking of them in their proper enjoyment (for instance, sex within the context of marriage). But I believe that there is a profound association between humility and the enjoyment of life, including the pleasures of the body.

God has made us as bodily creatures, and our bodily existence is a good gift from him.[1] Pride, especially spiritual pride, tends to be contemptuous of the pleasures of the body. But humble people can gratefully receive them as gifts from God. There is even something about their proper enjoyment that is spiritually nourishing and conducive to humility.

Do you remember what Bilbo does after he remembers his smallness? He enjoys his pipe!

Embrace Weakness

One of the most powerful ways to grow in humility is to embrace situations that make you uncomfortable or exhibit

---

1   For a helpful book on this topic, see Sam Allberry, *What God Has to Say about Our Bodies: How the Gospel Is Good News for Our Physical Selves* (Wheaton, IL: Crossway, 2021).

your weakness. We all have certain situations in which we feel vulnerable—times when we are not in control or not at our best, or that draw out our weaknesses.

When you think about it, life is filled with such moments. Pastors spending time with other pastors who are much more "successful" than they are. Parents when kids disobey them in public. Introverts going to social events where they don't know anyone. Older people going to the doctor with a fear of getting bad news.

We all know the acute vulnerability of such situations, and it is tempting to seek to eliminate that feeling from our lives. But it is unfortunate when we avoid stepping outside our strengths. Embracing weakness and vulnerability is a profound way to learn humility. It teaches us to rely on others. It reminds us that we don't have to be good at everything. It helps us find our identity not in our skills and gifts, but rather in the gospel.

It is wonderful to be able to say, "I'm not very good at this, and that is okay. I will do it anyway."

Laugh at Yourself

There are ways to laugh at yourself that should be avoided. As we have said, humility is never self-contempt or self-shaming.

On the other hand, there is a way to laugh at yourself that is healthy and life-giving. We all do things that are preposterous. We all have quirks. We all are, in some way or another, a bit ridiculous. It's healthy and freeing not to take ourselves too seriously and not to worry too much about whether others notice our oddities.

In Lewis's *The Horse and His Boy*, the horse Bree is proud and vain. He doesn't believe that Aslan is actually a real, physical lion. He talks down to the other characters. He is overly worried about his physical appearance and whether other horses roll on their backs in Narnia. Then Aslan actually shows up and confronts him:

"Now, Bree," he said, "you poor, proud frightened Horse, draw near. Nearer still, my son. Do not dare not to dare. Touch me. Smell me. Here are my paws, here is my tail, these are my whiskers. I am a true Beast."

"Aslan," said Bree in a shaken voice, "I'm afraid I must be rather a fool."

"Happy the Horse who knows that while he is still young. Or the Human either."[2]

---

2   C. S. Lewis, *The Chronicles of Narnia* (New York: HarperCollins, 2001), 299.

Aslan's words here imply something striking: everyone is, by nature, foolish. The difference is simply whether you realize it when you're young or old!

It might sound harsh, but it makes sense when you think about it: sin is folly, and we are all sinners. All our lives we will be unlearning foolishness and not taking ourselves too seriously. The earlier we can start, the better!

Visit a Cemetery

Have you ever walked through a cemetery and read the names and dates on the tombstones? It sounds a bit morbid, I know. But doing so offers a healthy, vivid reminder of something that we know but often forget: everybody dies. All of the tombstones represent real people who had dreams, aspirations, fears, and goals.

Some years ago, I was preaching through James and found myself deeply gripped by James 4:14: "What is your life? For you are a mist that appears for a little time and then vanishes."

Have you ever walked out on a cold night, exhaled, and noticed how long your breath lasts? According to the Bible, that is us. What a humbling thought! Regularly taking stock of our life like this is profoundly humbling. "Teach us to number our days / that we may get a heart of wisdom" (Ps. 90:12).

But strikingly, the fact that life is a vapor is not a reason to despair or to reject our existence as pointless. On the contrary, the tilt of Scripture's outlook is like this: *your life is a vapor, so enjoy it!*

This is part of the emphasis of Ecclesiastes. The book humbles us under the inescapable vanity of life. "All is vanity" is the recurrent theme. Yet it also claims:

- "Behold, what I have seen to be good and fitting is to eat and drink and find enjoyment in all the toil with which one toils under the sun the few days of his life that God has given him, for this is his lot" (Eccles. 5:18).
- "Go, eat your bread with joy, and drink your wine with a merry heart, for God has already approved what you do" (Eccles. 9:7).
- "Enjoy life with the wife whom you love, all the days of your vain life that he has given you under the sun, because that is your portion in life and in your toil at which you toil under the sun" (Eccles. 9:9).

Understanding the ephemeral nature of our lives helps us grow in humility and embrace each moment to the hilt for the vapor that it is.

Study the Universe

This one just never gets old. I've given up trying to describe how absolutely tiny I am and how absolutely massive is the world God made, because the words *tiny* and *massive* seem so inadequate. But making the effort to study this is still worth it.

So if you have twelve minutes to spare, search for "If the earth was a golf ball Louie Giglio" at YouTube.com and let your mind be blown.

I absolutely love Louie's words at 11:22: "When you see this, I don't know what happens to you, but I will tell you what happens to me. A shrinking feeling comes over me. And it's not a bad shrinking feeling. It's a good shrinking feeling."

Have you ever felt this *good shrinking feeling*? This feeling is part of being on the pathway of humility.

Meditate on Heavenly Worship

Whenever I find myself struggling, for whatever reason, to enter into corporate worship, I have developed a practice that helps me: remember the angels' heavenly worship of the ascended Christ that is happening *right now*. Even if the song I am hearing is cheesy or my heart is sluggish, it's rare that this thought doesn't help my perspective.

The reality of heavenly worship is always a powerful reminder. It has a wonderful way of putting earthly things in perspective. Consider that right now the mighty angels are bowing down in adoration, and that one day every knee will bow before the Lord Jesus. This puts both our accomplishments and our struggles in their proper context.

It's more difficult to think too much of yourself when you remember what is currently riveting the attention of the mightiest angels.

Bathe Everything Else in Humility

The early church theologian Basil of Caesarea preached a famous homily on humility. One of its great themes is that humility is the great converse of the human fall. The fall was caused by pride and resulted in the loss of our created glory. In contrast, the return to God is caused by humility and results in our heavenly glory.

After speaking of the fall of humanity, Basil wrote, "And now his surest salvation, the healing of his wound, his way of return to his beginning, is to be humble; not to think that he can ever of himself put on the cloak of glory, but that he must seek it from God."[3]

3 Basil the Great, Homily 20.1, "On Humility," http://www.lectionarycentral.com.

Basil thought of humility like a medicine to our deepest and realest need—"the healing of his wound." This is why it is the pathway to joy. Since the essence of all sin is pride, the essence of all progress against sin must always be humility. Humility is the remedy to what is most deeply wrong with us.

Therefore, just as pride permeates our lives and affects all that we do, so should humility. Humility is more than simply one more virtue to aim at—it is to be the atmosphere and quality in which we experience all of life. Humility is not just another thing to do: it is the way we should do everything.

Thus, humility is a whole new way of approaching life: an acceptance of our status as sinful and yet loved in the gospel, and consequently a self-forgetful, unpretentious bounce in our step that lives life to the full, embracing it as a wonderful gift from God.

O Lord, teach us how to pursue true humility that honors you. Give us courage to embrace those vulnerable places where we must rely fully on you. Give us freedom to enjoy the life you have given us to the full. Give us ears to hear, eyes to see, hearts that are grateful. May everything we do be bathed in humility: toward others, the world you have made, and most of all, you.

Discussion Questions

1. Which of the ten strategies mentioned in this chapter resonates most with you? Why?

2. What other practices in your life have you found helpful for cultivating humility?

PART 2

Cultivating Humility in Our Church Life

4

Humility in Leadership

Creating a Culture of Freedom

THE LAST FEW YEARS HAVE EXPOSED numerous instances of abuse by church leaders. It is impossible to articulate the amount of damage such episodes inflict upon people. When an enemy hurts you, that is bad; but when the *church* hurts you, the pain and disorientation are next-level.

It is tempting to think that church bullies are simply malicious people. But it's often more complicated than that. Many of them start out with good motives. Often they are gradually led into oppressive behavior through a long series of seemingly small steps of pride.

So much serious sin—abuse, bullying, intimidation— ultimately traces back to a lack of humility. In fact, here is a sobering truth: *anyone* can become a bully. It is naive to think that it could never happen to us. Stress and suffering can sour any of us—all it takes is for us to start walking by the flesh rather than the Spirit.

I'd put it this strongly: if you are in a position of authority, you will become either a servant or a bully. Your authority will be experienced by others as either freedom or oppression, depending on whether it is marked by humility.

How do we create a culture of freedom rather than oppression? Let's consider five strategies.

Choose to Trust Others

When you are a leader, it is so easy to be threatened by others who have gifts that you lack. For instance, imagine you are the senior pastor, but the congregation responds more enthusiastically when the assistant pastor preaches. You sense the energy in the room. You hear the buzz after the sermon.

If you are a leader, you will have *something* like this, and such circumstances will test whether your leadership creates a healthy or oppressive culture. In the case of the example above, it will be oh so easy to drop a comment here or there to minimize the assistant pastor or perhaps not let him preach at all (but then, you will have to make up a reason—and that is where you can become a bully).

No ministry can flourish like that. If you start down that path, where will it end? You will build a culture that is about *you* rather than a culture where others can flourish and find themselves. You must strive to be unthreatened when those under your leadership outshine you.

One of the keys to this is simply *choosing to trust others*. I know this is difficult, especially for those of us who have had our trust betrayed. And, granted, this does not mean blind trust. For example, if you are a senior pastor and you become aware that the assistant pastor is undermining you and seeking to gain undue influence among the elders, you have to address that. But when the assistant pastor is *not* doing that—when he simply preaches well—you must steer your heart away from the fear that his gifting will undermine you. Relax into the vulnerability of choosing to trust. Err on the side of gullibility rather than cynicism. Do not overprotect yourself.

In order to do this, we must have our identity rooted in the gospel. When your security comes from Christ, you can be free even to encourage the assistant pastor in his wonderful preaching gift. Build him up. Make it your personal goal to help him flourish and advance as much as you can.

If you are a leader and you are not regularly feeling vulnerable because of how much authority you are giving away—

how much trust you are placing in others—you are probably not leading with humility.

Rely on Those around You

A related temptation is to try to do all the work ourselves. This is a recipe for burnout, and it stems from pride. Humble leaders are happy to delegate. They don't have a hand in everything. They know it's not about them, and they also know that they simply aren't good at everything.

This means *accepting that others will function differently from you* and genuinely being okay with that. If the differences are not clear matters of morality, you must simply accept that others are different. Therefore:

- Let the elder who is leading the elders meeting actually lead it, even if his method of leading is less efficient from your standpoint. Resist the temptation to break in and control the conversation.
- Let the youth pastor have a messy office.
- Let the worship leader be more casual than you.

Not everyone has to do things just like you would do them. Offer correctives when you need to for clear problems, but most of the time, let people learn on their own. Just because you are the leader doesn't mean you don't need to flex and adjust to others. You also are part of a larger system, to which you must submit.

One practical way I have found helpful to rely on others as a pastor is working through teams. If you are going to rework your bylaws, commission a group to oversee the process. If you are going to hire someone, set up a search committee. Working through a team is less efficient and can be threatening because you are no longer in control. (What if the team disagrees with you?) But it is a healthy practice, I believe, especially for large-scale decisions and processes.

Working through a team creates a natural accountability. It allows for diverse perspectives to influence the process and outcome. It builds a sense of shared ownership and investment among the team for whatever the outcome is. It helps gain the trust of those outside the team. And it even provides an opportunity for leadership development and recruitment among the members of the team. (You might discover a future elder in the process.)[1]

Create an Environment of Encouragement

Encouragement is one of the most powerful tools we have as leaders. And we have the ability not only to use it ourselves,

1   Portions of this paragraph and the next section are adapted from my article "Keep Learning to Lead: Five Practical Lessons," Desiring God, February 23, 2017, https://www.desiringgod.org/articles/.

but to influence the whole *culture* we are leading to a climate of encouragement. Whatever the leadership is, the rest of the institution eventually becomes—so if you are regularly encouraging people, others will notice and be influenced to do the same.

One of the things I have tried to build into my weekly schedule is deliberate encouragement to others. Often it's something simple, like a quick text message or email. Even a small gesture like this that takes only thirty seconds of your day can make a difference for someone. (We just have to be intentional about remembering to do it.)

When I do this, I am amazed at how frequently someone writes back to say something like "This came at exactly the right time" or "I really needed to hear that today." I've concluded that *most* people, *most* of the time, need encouragement. It is so important to remember this in the way we lead and shepherd others.

Too often, we conceive of leadership as primarily corrective, with occasional encouragement. It should be the exact opposite. Encouragement should be the norm. Correction should be sparing.

One way to try to build this into the culture you are leading is to create times for intentional encouragement. During a meeting, for instance, give people an opportunity to say something kind to build up or express appreciation to another person present. There are ways to do this that can feel forced or cheesy, but it's been amazing to me to consider the impact that it has. Try it out and see for yourself.

Another way to build a culture of encouragement is to celebrate "success stories." For instance, when a layperson in the church shares the gospel with his neighbor, ask him to share his experience with the rest of the church. Or when a volunteer is faithfully serving in the nursery, highlight her service publicly in order to help the church value this calling as important and Christ honoring. Regularly honor others for their hard work.

Celebrating how God is at work in this way has several wonderful results. It affirms a person in his or her service. It encourages and motivates others who are serving in similar ways. (They think, "Wow, what I am doing matters!") It teaches others to follow the person's example. (They say to themselves, "I can do that too!") It reinforces that the ministry is not carried out only by the leaders, but that every person matters. And it has a wonderfully positive effect on the overall morale of the group.

Correct with Gentleness

Although it's true that leadership is not *primarily* corrective, it's also true that effective leadership must involve correction at times. When a leader is unwilling or afraid to address problems, sin and dysfunction fester. This means we have to be willing to have hard conversations and even take disciplinary action when necessary.

When we correct others, we must do so in a spirit of gentleness. Gentleness is not weakness: it is strength under control. It is how Christ treats us when we need correction: "He can deal gently with the ignorant and wayward" (Heb. 5:2).

How do we offer correctives with gentleness? First, give correction in person. It is far easier to be ungentle in an email. Being with someone causes you to feel more vulnerable, and this helps soften your approach. Second, frame correction in the context of encouragement as much as possible (for instance, "You did a great job, but you can make it even more effective by . . ."). I know this might sound corny, but it works! Third, remember what it feels like to be corrected. It can be embarrassing and even painful. Seek to be as understated and gracious as you can. Have sympathy for the person being corrected. Don't be overbearing. As soon as the person gets the point, move on.

Also, remember that the primary way your leadership will correct others is not through your words, but through your example. Peter describes how elders are to exhibit authority to those under their care: "not domineering over those in your charge, but being examples to the flock" (1 Pet. 5:3).

It's interesting that for Peter, the alternative to a domineering style of leadership is *being an example*. Isn't this profoundly humbling? It means our primary focus should always be on ourselves. For every minute you spend thinking about what needs to be corrected in someone else, you should spend many more minutes thinking about what needs to be corrected in yourself.

Be Willing to Apologize

It is easy to think of leadership as primarily telling others what to do. Actually, leadership has far more to do with our *own* actions. For example, leaders must model repentance. We must be the chief repenters, the first to soften in a conflict, the most willing to apologize and make things right. This will make you feel vulnerable, but it is what true leadership is all about.

Being a parent of four young children has helped me learn this. Sometimes I find myself about to offer a correction, and then I suddenly stop and think, "This doesn't really merit a correction—I just need to chill out." At other times, it suddenly occurs to me that I'm being impatient or ungentle, and—however much that feeling of impatience might seem justified—it is, in fact, wrong. It is humbling as a parent to recognize such things and have to own up to them.

But the most wonderful and amazing lesson I've learned is that when I apologize to my kids, *they are so willing to forgive me!* Things immediately get better. Simple, powerful words like these can do wonders: "Isaiah, I was being impatient just now. I'm sorry. Will you forgive me?" I believe that being willing to say that to my children influences the culture of my family for good far more than any brilliant parenting advice I could offer.

If we are not willing to apologize, why should we expect that those under our care will? If we are not modeling repentance to others, why should we expect them to know how to do it?

If you are a leader, freely acknowledge your mistakes to those under your care. When you are wrong, don't say, "Yeah, but what I *really* meant was . . ." (Have you noticed how often people do this?) Instead, say, "I was wrong."

Genuinely humble yourself before others. *If you do that, people will respond.* You will be blown away by the impact such humbling will have and the freedom it will create.

Lord Jesus, you are our model in all this. You are the servant leader who stooped to wash the disciples' feet. You gave up your rights and took the lowest place. O Lord, help us to shepherd those under our care as you shepherd us. Teach us to lead with humility and love, as you have done for us.

Discussion Questions

1. What are some situations as a leader that you find threatening? What do you think it looks like to respond to them with humility?

2. Has someone in a leadership position over you ever apologized to you? What effect did it have on you?

3. Who are some people in your life who need encouragement? What are some practical ways you can encourage them?

5

Humility among Peers

Overcoming Envy and Competition

THIS CHAPTER IS ABOUT showing humility toward our peers—the people in our lives who are neither under our authority (our children, for instance) nor in a position of authority over us (a pastor or boss, for example).

So this is potentially the most broadly applicable of these final three chapters. In a church context, this includes all the other members in the church; and if you're a pastor, it includes other pastors as well.

In peer relationships, the particular form that pride often takes is *envy*. This isn't the only way that pride can manifest itself, of course, but it is a particularly common one, so it is worth reflecting on it a bit.

Why Envy Is a Particularly Deadly Sin

Some years ago, I preached a sermon on envy. I had never really thought in depth about envy before, so it was fascinating to study this particular vice. It was also terrifying.

We typically think of pride as the chief of the vices and the opposite of humility, and that is right. C. S. Lewis called pride "the essential vice" and wrote, "It was through Pride that the devil became the devil: Pride leads to every other vice: it is the complete anti-God state of mind."[1] Similarly, Jonathan Edwards wrote that pride is "the first sin that ever entered into the universe and the last that is rooted out. It is God's most stubborn enemy!"[2]

But envy is closely related to pride and stands near it, close to the very essence of evil. We might think of pride as the root of evil, and of envy as one of its necessary and immediate fruits, particularly in how it manifests itself toward our peers.

What is envy, exactly? It is typically understood as an unpleasant and resentful feeling toward someone else's advantage. I like Thomas Aquinas's brief and insightful definition of envy as "sorrow for another's good."[3]

1 C. S. Lewis, *Mere Christianity*, in *The Complete C. S. Lewis Signature Classics* (San Francisco: HarperSanFrancisco, 2002), 103

2 *The Works of Jonathan Edwards*, ed. Edward Hickman (Edinburgh: Banner of Truth, 1979), 1:398–99.

3 Thomas Aquinas, *Summa Theologica* II, Q. 36, trans. Fathers of the English Dominican Province (Notre Dame, IN: Christian Classics, 1948).

Just think for a moment about how squarely *malicious* envy is based on this definition. In fact, just as pride is the opposite of humility, envy can be thought of as the opposite of love. Love says, "I'm happy when you're happy, and I'm sad when you're sad." Envy says, "I'm happy when you're sad, and I'm sad when you're happy." Could anything be more terrible?

There are two other reasons why, of all sins, envy is a particularly deadly one.

First, envy is more subtle and invisible than other sins. If you are struggling with murderous thoughts toward someone, you usually at least know what you are struggling with. But it is possible to be completely consumed with envy and not have a clue. It hides in our hearts. Like pride, the more we succumb to it, the more blind we become to its effect on us. The worst sins often are like that.

Second, envy is one of the most miserable vices. Most other vices tend to produce some kind of pleasure, however momentary. But envy is nothing but unpleasant, through and through. It is the constant thief of joy.

Imagine that you win the lottery. Are you happy? Not if you have envy. Envy will immediately come in and say, "But look how much the government took. And so-and-so still has a bigger house than I do. Why did I not win as much as that other person?" And so forth.

There is no joy in your life that cannot be destroyed by envy. No matter what you have, envy can say, "Yes, you might have X, but you don't have Y."

Have you heard this voice before, in your heart?

- "Yeah, you might have gotten into that college, but you didn't get into *that* one."
- "Yeah, you might be making good money, but you don't have enough time to enjoy it."
- "Yeah, your church might be growing, but you don't have the opportunities that so-and-so has." (Yes, ministers have thoughts like this; unfortunately, we are very prone to envy.)

The ultimate expression of envy came in the garden of Eden. Adam and Eve were literally in paradise, but envy came along and said, "Yeah, you may be in paradise, but you're not God." *There is no heaven that envy cannot make into a hell.* It blinds and distorts how we experience heaven itself. As Derek Kidner put it, "There is nothing so blinding as envy or grievance. This was the nerve the serpent touched in Eden, to make even paradise appear an insult."[4]

---

4   Derek Kidner, *Psalms 73–150* (Downers Grove, IL: IVP Academic, 1975), 291.

I am going on about this because I believe that envy is a huge source of misery in our lives, often in ways we are not fully aware of. I think it especially lurks on social media, where we are constantly tempted to compare ourselves to others.

I want us to see this so that we can understand just how crucial humility is to a life of joy. Humility is how we battle envy. Therefore, there could not be more at stake in the struggle between humility and envy going on in our hearts. It is as fierce and decisive as the battle between heaven and hell.

So what does it look like, practically, to fight against feelings of envy and instead pursue humility? Here are four strategies.

Feast upon the Gospel

First, you must fill your heart with the riches of Christ's love. You must let the wonders of the gospel seep down into every nook and cranny of your soul. You must let his love, his joy, and his goodness flow into you at the deepest level possible, meeting the needs and desires that cause us to struggle with envy. But what specifically does that look like?

Imagine that there is a little garden outside your house where it is wonderfully quiet. The flowers spread a beautiful fragrance. The birds are chirping there, and the air is fresh. Whenever life is stressful, you can walk into the garden and clear your mind for a few moments. It is a place of comfort and refuge for you.

Whatever else is happening, you know you can retreat into the garden to restore your emotional well-being.

This is the role of the gospel for a Christian. It is your place of retreat, your refuge, the garden into which you can enter for restoration. It is free, always there, and sufficient to meet your need.

We learn how this works in Psalm 73. What a comfort that the writers of Scripture spoke so honestly about the struggle with envy! This is Asaph's struggle in this psalm: "I was envious of the arrogant / when I saw the prosperity of the wicked" (73:3). He goes on and on about how easy wicked people's lives are and how successful they appear, despite their arrogance and cruelty (73:4–12). He even gets to the point of feeling that his integrity is a waste (73:13).

How did Asaph get over his envy? In part, he had to learn of the true fate of the wicked (73:18–20). This is also helpful for us to know when we envy the wicked. But the ultimate resolution comes from his newfound awareness of what God means to him:

> Nevertheless, I am continually with you;
>> you hold my right hand.
> You guide me with your counsel,
>> and afterward you will receive me to glory.

Whom have I in heaven but you?
   And there is nothing on earth that I desire
      besides you.
My flesh and my heart may fail,
   but God is the strength of my heart and my portion
      forever. (73:23–26)

For us as well, the remedy to envy is finding contentment in God. In the gospel, God has given you his very self. He is your portion. He is the great goal of your life. You will be with him in glory forever. And throughout all your days in this life, he is with you continually, guiding you, holding you by the hand.

Set your heart upon this. Let it really land on you amid your current struggles. Pray Psalm 73:23–26 over and over to the Lord, and ask him to make it real to your heart.

Remember Who Your Real Enemy Is

Envy produces feelings of competitiveness among us and our peers. I think this is especially the case among pastors and those in ministry. Tragically, I suspect it is very common.

For example, a pastor can feel threatened by how much more gifted another pastor is or how much bigger his church is. Or he might wonder, "How does he have that many Twitter followers?" Or he might see the impact that someone else is having and question why God isn't pouring out a similar blessing on his own ministry.

One powerful way to combat these unpleasant feelings is to remember that all of those who are serving Christ are ultimately on the same team. I've often been struck by the fact that what immediately precedes the list of spiritual gifts in Romans 12 is Paul's injunction to humility: "I say to everyone among you not to think of himself more highly than he ought to think" (12:3). What does humility have to do with spiritual gifts?

I think the answer comes in what follows: "For as in one body we have many members, and the members do not all have the same function, so we, though many, are one body in Christ, and individually members one of another" (Rom. 12:4–5). Humility flows from seeing ourselves in the context of the body of Christ. We are all members of one body, each with our own particular roles to play.

Since we are all on the same team, that other pastor is *not* my enemy. He is my brother. We both have a common enemy: Satan. There is something about remembering the spiritual realm, and the battle that is taking place there between the forces of light and the forces of darkness, that is wonderfully clarifying and sobering. It helps us see where the real battle lies.

If you are a pastor, think about this: the minister you envy is on Satan's list. Satan wants to take him down. Doesn't this help change your perspective a bit? Doesn't it help you more easily root for his success?

Pray for God's Blessing on Those You Are Tempted to Envy

The composer and conductor Leonard Bernstein was once asked which musical instrument is most difficult to play. He reputedly answered, "Second fiddle. I can get plenty of first violinists, but to find someone who can play the second fiddle with enthusiasm—that's a problem. And if we have no second fiddle, we have no harmony."[5]

How powerfully insightful for life! The world is filled with people vying to play first violin. But can we play the second fiddle with enthusiasm? Finding our own unique role and being content in it—this is where flourishing happens. This is where life gets interesting. This is where the joy comes out.

---

5 Cited in Charles Swindoll, "Playing Second Fiddle," Insight for Living Ministries, January 14, 2021, https://insight.org.

One way we can pursue this is to pray for God's blessings on others. Sincerely wish good for the first violinists who are in the spotlight. Ask God to make them flourish.

This is difficult! You might say, "But I don't want God's blessing on them!" Ah, but do you *want* to want it? Our prayers can shape our desires. The more you pray for God's blessing on someone, the more the tentacles of envy around your heart are weakened.

My brother Dane recently wrote an outstanding book (I'm guessing you've heard of it!) entitled *Gentle and Lowly*.[6] Hopefully by this point you've picked up on the fact that I'm not Dane—but if you bought this book because you thought I was him, I am glad you have made it this far!

By God's grace, I don't think I have particularly struggled with envy over the success of Dane's book. But I wanted to make sure early on that I wouldn't get anywhere near envy, because I thought it might be a temptation.

So I made a practice, every time I heard about how God had used Dane's book, to pray that God would use it even more. (I can pray this sincerely because it's such a fantastic book.) Every time I hear about how many copies have been

6   Dane C. Ortlund, *Gentle and Lowly: The Heart of Christ for Sinners and Sufferers* (Wheaton, IL: Crossway, 2020).

sold, I pray even more will sell. I pray that the book will keep on selling until every person on earth has five copies, and then we can start shipping them into outer space to bless the aliens.

Can you pray for God's blessings on those you are tempted to envy? Of course, this will look different for different people. If the people you envy are the wicked people Asaph was describing in Psalm 73, then you won't really pray for "blessing" on them in the same sense. You could pray, though, for the blessing of their salvation.

But tragically, so much of the time, we envy other brothers and sisters in Christ. When we are tempted to this, praying for God's blessing on their lives can help us replace feelings of envy with feelings of friendship, encouragement, and goodwill.

Lord, help us learn to play second fiddle with enthusiasm!

Make the Glory of Christ Your Chief Aim

Corrie ten Boom was once asked if it was difficult for her to be humble. She reputedly replied,

When Jesus rode into Jerusalem on Palm Sunday on the back of a donkey, and everyone was waving palm branches and throwing garments onto the road, and singing praises, do you think that for one moment it ever entered the head

67

of that donkey that any of that was for him? If I can be the donkey on which Jesus Christ rides in his glory, I give him all the praise and all the honor.[7]

This is a wonderful image to keep in mind, especially for those of us in ministry. We are just the donkey! We are not building our own kingdom or fame, but that of Christ. Our lives should mean nothing to us except to serve as a vehicle for his praise, glory, and renown.

This might seem threatening or dismaying. But it shouldn't! We should not hear this calling to serve the glory of Christ as bad news! It is so much more wonderful to serve his cause than our own! Pursuing our own glory is pathetic and boring. But seeking the glory of Jesus Christ is the most thrilling, enthralling adventure you could ever spend your life on.

Just consider that right now in heaven all the saints and angels are worshiping the risen Christ. All heaven is roaring with praise. It is the ultimate rock concert, and it will never end. And what is the word that they keep repeating in Revelation 5? *Worthy*.

---

7   This quotation is often repeated and attributed to Corrie ten Boom, but I am unable to identify a source for it.

"Worthy is the Lamb who was slain, to receive power and wealth and wisdom and might and honor and glory and blessing!" (Rev. 5:12).

I love this word. I often come back to it in my worship. Christ is *worthy* of our worship. Does this word land on your heart? It means that what Christ has accomplished is such that if we do not worship him, if we do not serve his glory, we commit an injustice. Glory is what he is due. Do you remember Christ's rebuke to the Pharisees at the triumphal entry? If the people did not praise him, Jesus said, "the very stones would cry out" (Luke 19:40). Jesus *must* be praised.

Why is this? Think about what he has done. He came down into our world as one of us and suffered the worst death imaginable. Then he triumphed over evil forever in the most stunning victory the world has ever known. It's the greatest story ever told. It's the most thrilling drama ever imagined.

This is the cause we are a part of! This is the one we serve— the one every creature was *born* to worship, the one before whom every knee will bow and every tongue confess one day (Phil. 2:10–11).

If you let this reality fill your heart, you will find that it's harder to feel threatened by the successful church across town. The brothers and sisters there are contributing to the same wonderful cause we are, the glory of Jesus Christ (if it is a faithful church, that is). As lay Christians, focusing on the glory of Christ can help us root for Christians in a different tribe, even if they have different views on some nonessential doctrines.

There is joy in embracing the fact that *it's not about us.* It reminds us what we are really fighting for.

Lord, help us embrace these words and know them as joyful words: it's not about us. Give us a sense of the splendor of your glory. Teach us the joy and freedom of spending our lives to make you known, and unite our hearts together with everyone else serving this wonderful cause!

You're Nobody Very Special, and That's Okay

Earlier we mentioned the character Bree in C. S. Lewis's *The Horse and His Boy.* Bree is a talking Narnian horse who has been taken captive, and therefore has lived all his life among horses that cannot speak. As a result, he has come to think that he is particularly strong and brave. However, on one occasion, he is humiliated when he shows cowardice in a moment of danger. He is despondent, declares that he has lost everything, and wonders whether he should return to slavery rather than go back to Narnia. The old hermit the horses are staying with overhears him and rebukes him:

My good Horse, you've lost nothing but your self-conceit. No, no, cousin. Don't put back your ears and shake your mane at me. If you are really so humbled as you sounded a minute ago, you must learn to listen to sense. You're not quite the great Horse you had come to think, from living among poor dumb horses. Of course you were braver and cleverer than *them*. You could hardly help being that. It doesn't follow that you'll be anyone very special in Narnia. But as long as you know you're nobody very special, you'll be a very decent sort of Horse, on the whole, and taking one thing with another.[8]

I like these words: *as long as you know you're nobody very special.*

In the places where we are very ordinary, or even below average, we need not panic. Mediocrity is not the end of the world. Your value is rooted in what Christ has done for you. You are loved and treasured by God himself. Your life is measured by his estimation. You have an ocean of joy awaiting you in eternity. So your happiness and welfare are not dependent on being a big deal.

8   C. S. Lewis, *The Chronicles of Narnia* (New York: HarperCollins, 2001), 275.

71

Therefore, you can move among your peers with freedom, offering your best contribution for whatever it is, and appreciating theirs in return. The important thing is not your contribution, but the larger work you are a part of.

It is one of the most wonderful moments of life when you are able to say, and really mean it from your heart, "I'm nobody very special—and that's okay!"

Discussion Questions

1. What effect have you seen envy have in your life or in someone else's life?

2. What influence does social media have on envy? How specifically have you seen this?

3. What strategy (drawn from this chapter or elsewhere) have you found useful for fighting envy?

6

Humility toward Leaders

Understanding What Submission Really Means

THIS CHAPTER IS ABOUT humility toward leaders, with a special view to the context of the local church. We have looked at humility toward those under us in terms of creating a culture of freedom, and we have considered humility to our peers in terms of fighting envy. Here we consider humility toward those in leadership over us as an act of *submission*.

This is an especially delicate topic these days for the reason we identified at the start of chapter 4—there have been so many abuses by church leaders. Many people have been wounded by the church, perhaps so much so that they may not feel they have the patience to even *listen* to any talk about submission.

I can sympathize with this worry. I myself have been wounded by the misuse of spiritual authority. I know that feeling. It is terrible. It is probably the deepest pain in my life. So the last thing I want to do is minimize concern about the misuse of spiritual authority.

In fact, let me create a little breathing room right up front: submission to authority does not mean blind acceptance or passive reception of whatever the leadership says or does. On the contrary, we submit to leaders as an act of submission to God. Therefore, when a leader in the church deviates from God's word or God's will, we must submit to the Lord *rather* than to that leader. This means we must practice spiritual discernment in how we relate to our leaders. No one is beyond accountability.

Let me put it as clearly as I can: *we should not submit to abuse.* Never, never, never.

At the same time, there *is* such a thing as healthy submission to authority. For instance, in Scripture we read,

- "We ask you, brothers, to respect those who labor among you and are over you in the Lord and admonish you, and to esteem them very highly in love because of their work" (1 Thess. 5:12–13).

- "Obey your leaders and submit to them, for they are keeping watch over your souls, as those who will have to give an account" (Heb. 13:17).

Therefore, while firmly opposing the abuse of power, we should not reject all expressions of church authority. I often worry that the tragic reality of domineering pastors will undermine all confidence in the pastoral office, making the jobs of faithful, godly pastors that much harder.

So it is imperative for us to think about this question: What does humility toward leadership look like?

All Submission Is Directed to God

To begin with, submission won't make much sense if you aren't practicing it first and foremost to God. The act of becoming a Christian is itself an act of submission. We submit both to God's assessment of our sins and to his remedy for our condition.

And throughout the entire Christian life, we must continually submit to God, over and over. As the first of Martin Luther's Ninety-Five Theses states, "When our Lord and Master Jesus Christ said, 'Repent' (Mt 4:17), he willed the entire life of believers to be one of repentance."[1]

---

1   "The 95 Theses," https://www.luther.de/en/95thesen.html.

This is the entire atmosphere of the Christian life: constant course corrections as we respond to God's word, as the Holy Spirit nudges us, and as we learn from other believers. And all of this is *submission*: accepting something you otherwise would not choose. It means turning, changing, adjusting. It means saying to God, as Christ modeled for us so poignantly, "Not what I will, but what you will" (Mark 14:36).

All other submission in our lives should flow from this foundation. We do not submit to leaders because we fear *them*: we submit to leaders because we fear *God*. If we can embrace this dynamic, everything else about submission will go more smoothly.

(By the way, if you have never submitted to God by accepting the gospel, you can do so right now by praying a prayer like this: *Lord, I confess that I have sinned against you. Please forgive me. I accept Christ's work on the cross for me. I surrender my life to you. Teach me how to follow you. Amen.*)

Submission in Worship

We often think of the singing part of a church service as the worship. But in reality, everything in the service is a part of the worship—even listening to the sermon. Remember, we are hearing the very word of God!

Here are two simple ways you can worship during the sermon:

- When you hear something that is convicting, immediately repent before the Lord.
- When you hear something that is encouraging or uplifting, immediately give thanks to the Lord.

Don't wait till after the sermon is over. Receive it—insofar as it is faithful to God's word—as God speaking to you right there in the pew. And talk back to him during the sermon (whether out loud or not will depend on your church tradition!).

Be the Kind of Person Who Can Receive Correction

As we have seen, one short definition of humility is "teachableness." A humble person is capable of being instructed. Being taught requires humility because it requires admitting you don't yet know that which you are learning.

No matter how old we are, how much we've studied, or how much experience we have, we will always be learning and growing. Therefore, we must remain teachable for our entire lives. Interestingly, we often learn the most from unlikely sources—from people we are tempted to look down on or people who are very different from us. I have been astonished at how much we can continually learn from children, for example.

We might think of receiving correction or being taught as coming in a formal context, such as an official rebuke or church discipline. But those are the exceptional and extreme cases. So much of humility is receiving correction before it gets to that point. A humble person is *constantly* receiving input from others in all kinds of informal ways—a mere casual remark or even a quizzical look might be the occasion for correction and teaching.

The idea is that you want to be the kind of person who is generally *responsive* to leadership. You want to be the kind of person to whom it is easy to give advice, who really listens to and values others' feedback.

Do you remember how Hebrews 13:17 continues after calling us to submit to leaders as they watch over our souls? It says, "Let them do this with joy and not with groaning, for that would be of no advantage to you."

When we are teachable, we make our pastor's job a joy. So here is a wonderful prayer to come back to: *Lord, help me be the kind of person who is a joy for my pastor to have at church.*

Don't Grumble about Decisions

I heard recently that after COVID-19, a majority of pastors would leave the ministry if they could. This is a real problem in the church right now. We need our shepherds!

Sadly, there are many domineering, abusive pastors out there, as we have mentioned. But this should not cause us to reject the many good-hearted, imperfect pastors who are genuinely seeking to serve Christ. You need to know that the way you treat your pastor really does deeply affect him and his family, and it is so important to be careful not to make his job any harder than it already is.

There are doubtless many reasons why so many pastors are discouraged right now. The whole COVID-19 season has been brutal for pastors. And Satan surely targets them. But tragically, sometimes the shepherd gets mistreated by the very sheep he is seeking to care for. Church members can wound or discourage their pastors through harsh criticism, complaining, unrealistic expectations, lack of commitment, and much more.

So part of submission to your leaders is accepting their leadership without grumbling, gossip, general negativity, or defiance. Of course, there are times to make your opinion known to the leaders, especially if it is on a critical doctrinal or moral matter. But don't constantly question everything they do. Try to be supportive whenever you can. On balance, make it your general approach to *embrace their vision and leadership*.

In other words, don't say, "I will support the leadership if I have a good reason to." Instead, say, "I will joyfully support the leadership unless I have a good reason *not* to." Do you see the difference? It's a matter of your default posture.

Along the way, appreciate how difficult your pastor's job is, as is the job of the other leaders in the church. They are almost always facing far more than you realize or can see. Fight against an "I know better" attitude. Trust me, the job is a lot harder than it looks!

And remember: encourage your pastor as much as you can, and pray for him (and his family). I can almost guarantee you he needs both your encouragement and prayers.

Father, we pray for our shepherds. Strengthen them. Encourage them. Sustain them. Help us to be a joy to them, not a source of groaning.

For the One Whose Submission Was Abused

As I have written this chapter, I've frequently thought of those who will read this book and have been mistreated by others with an appeal to "submission." Please know I appreciate how difficult this topic must be for you. I get it. I've been there.

So let me reiterate for maximal clarity that submission never means accepting abuse. If your husband is violent toward you, you should not submit to that. Instead, you should tell a trusted friend who can help you take appropriate steps to protect yourself, such as notifying the authorities. Likewise, if your pastor is a bully, you don't need to stay at the church and be bullied. Instead, you should prayerfully seek a healthy church, as God leads you and you are able. If you are a pastor and your elders are cruel and dishonest, you don't need to submit to their false narratives. Instead, you should address what is happening with as much wisdom as you can muster and seek to create a culture of leadership in your church that is good and righteous. If you cannot do it—if they fire you and slander you—then you have *not* failed to submit to leadership. Your conscience is clear before God.

If you have been victim of the misuse of authority, let me say three things to you from my heart:

1. What happened to you was wrong. I am so sorry.
2. You are precious in the sight of God. Therefore, your safety and well-being are important to him. You are worth protecting.
3. Jesus will never treat you like that. He is kind. He is good. He is safe. You may need to distance yourself

from the one who hurt you in his name, but don't distance yourself from him. Run *to* him, not *from* him. You will find him the gentlest friend you could imagine. Indeed, he knows all too well what it is like to be mistreated, betrayed, slandered, and abused.

There's a scene in *The Magician's Nephew* where a little boy named Digory meets Aslan.[2] His mother is sick, and he wants to ask for Aslan's help, but he's afraid. Lewis writes:

Up till then he had been looking at the Lion's great front feet and the huge claws on them; now, in his despair, he looked up at its face. What he saw surprised him as much as anything in his whole life. For the tawny face was bent down near his own and (wonder of wonders) great shining tears stood in the Lion's eyes. They were such big, bright tears compared with Digory's own that for a moment he felt as if the Lion must really be sorrier about his Mother than he was himself. "My son, my son," said Aslan. "I know. Grief is great. Only you and I in this land know that yet. Let us be good to one another."

2   The conclusion to this chapter is adapted from my article "How Not to Help a Sufferer," The Gospel Coalition, February 18, 2017, https://www.thegospel coalition.org/.

What a world of comfort is bound up in those words, "I know." Jesus is the great sufferer, the man of sorrows. No one could ever suffer more, for he took on our sins and absorbed the full sting of justice on our behalf, sinking down into the depths of hell and forsakenness. Because of this, he is the *perfect* friend to sufferers. He could not be better suited, or better prepared, to heal your heart and meet your need. Go to him.

Discussion Questions

1. Suppose you have a concern with a decision made by the leadership of your church. How do you know if it is so important you should say something about it? What ways of articulating concerns have you found to be fruitful?

2. What ways have you found to be effective in encouraging your pastor?

Conclusion

Joy as the Acid Test of Humility

THROUGHOUT THIS BOOK, we've observed that humility is the pathway to joy. This was true for Christ himself—his humiliation and suffering ultimately led to joy (Heb. 12:2), as well as glory (Phil. 2:9–11). This is the paradigm for us all—humility, then joy; descent, then ascent; suffering, then glory.

Basil of Caesarea, in his wonderful homily on humility, put it like this:

Follow after humility, as a lover of it. Love it, and it will glorify you. If you wish to travel to the true glory, this is the way, with the angels, and with God. And in the presence of the angels Christ will acknowledge you as His disciple; and He will give you glory if you have imitated His humility.[1]

While the ultimate realization of this trajectory will come in heaven, humility is also the doorway to joy in each moment and scene of life. Humility is *inherently* cheerful and uplifting. I love how Augustine put it: "There is something in humility which, strangely enough, exalts the heart, and something in pride which debases it."[2] Similarly, Jonathan Edwards claimed that humility "tends to the purity of Christian feeling" and is "the source of some of the sweetest exercises of Christian experience."[3]

It's as though there are certain Christian experiences of loveliness and contentment that can be accessed only by humility—territories of joy we have not yet even imagined, to which humility is the only possible pathway.

At the end of the movie *It's a Wonderful Life*, the character George Bailey helps me understand this (spoiler coming in the rest of this paragraph and next). If you've seen the movie, you know the plot: he's been given a chance to discover what

1 Basil the Great, Homily 20.7, "On Humility," http://www.lectionarycentral.com.
2 Augustine, *The City of God* 14.13 (New York: Random House, 2010), 461.
3 Jonathan Edwards, *Charity and Its Fruits: Living in the Light of God's Love*, ed. Kyle Strobel (Wheaton, IL: Crossway, 2012), 159.

the world would have been like if he'd never been born. When he gets his life back, he is filled with gratitude for the wonder of being alive. All his financial problems seem insignificant.

Can you remember him running through town, jubilantly yelling, "Merry Christmas, Bedford Falls"? Can you picture him eagerly arriving home to his family, hugging and kissing his children? Suddenly the world has new magic. Even the broken knob on the stairway banister merits his affection.

This is a picture of what humility does. It opens us to the sheer wonder of being alive. What did we do to deserve it?

Humility can teach us to embrace each day with the fresh perspective of George Bailey. In the morning, when we sit down to eat our breakfast, we think, "Who am I, that I get to eat this wonderful food? What did I do to deserve it?" When we arrive at work, we think, "Who am I, that I get to contribute to this work? That I get to know these colleagues?" When we come home at the end of the day, we think, "Who am I to have this wonderful family, these friends, this house? To have this life?"

Of course, life is also difficult and filled with suffering. When a person is going through extreme suffering, I want to alleviate her from any undue pressure to try to cultivate an emotional response that would be unrealistic in that circumstance. She simply has my prayers and sympathy.

But most of us, in the ordinary course of life, should culti-vate wonder and gratitude at the miracle of being alive. Every day is a gift. There is no end to the wonder and joy of it.

George Bailey's exhilaration is a model for us all.

As you finish this book, just take a moment to thank God for your life. Review your blessings. Count as many of them as you can think of, and give deep thanks to God. You will find, I think, that it is almost impossible for a feeling of joy not to warm your heart.

God, who are we, that you have created us? You had no need of us. You were overflowing in love and joy already without us as Father, Son, and Spirit. But in your generosity, you have allowed us to share in that joy. Thank you. From the bottom of our hearts, we give you thanks. Lead us each day on the pathway toward joy, and toward yourself.

Epilogue

Humility in Social Media Engagement

SOCIAL MEDIA OFTEN SEEMS to reflect the opposite values of God's kingdom.[1]

Jesus said, "Blessed are the peacemakers" (Matt. 5:9). Social media often seems to bless the outraged. Jesus said, "Blessed are the meek" (5:5). Social media often seems to bless the narcissistic.

I'm grateful for many godly Christian leaders who model an edifying use of social media. At the same time, I worry that we as the church are often shaped by the unhealthy dynamics of social-media culture more than we are shaping it. Too often, we get pulled into the yuck, the noise, the sneering.

1 Portions of this epilogue are adapted from my article "3 Ways to Keep Social Media from Stealing Your Joy," The Gospel Coalition, May 2, 2020, https://www.thegospelcoalition.org/.

In particular, social media often steers us away from humility. Charles Spurgeon's rebuke could well apply to our social-media age:

> We have plenty of people nowadays who could not kill a mouse without publishing in the *Gospel Gazette*. Samson killed a lion and said nothing about it: the Holy Spirit finds modesty so rare that He takes care to record it. Say much of what the Lord has done for you, but say little of what you have done for the Lord. Do not utter a single self-glorifying sentence![2]

I am convicted by Spurgeon's words. How many times have I drawn attention to myself? How many times have I risked offending the Holy Spirit by breaching modesty or courtesy? *Lord, I am sorry.*

So what do we do? I don't think the answer is necessarily to avoid social media altogether, though it may be for some, and all of us should consider our limitations. But I do think that in the current state of our culture, godliness in social-media use requires extra intentionality and ballast.

2   Charles H. Spurgeon, "Hands Full of Honey," a sermon preached at the Metropolitan Tabernacle on January 28, 1883, www.spurgeon.org.

We will not likely drift into an edifying use of Twitter or Instagram. Things such as self-promotion and meanness are too powerful a current.

How do we build a social-media presence that is informed by humility? I'm still wrestling with what this looks like, but here are three strategies we might consider starting with.

Fight Envy with Gratitude

Social media invites constant comparison, making envy a constant danger. There will always be someone with more followers and some new crisis you feel you must weigh in on (or a joke you want to be a part of). It's easy for the fear of being overlooked to become a tyrant or the need to maintain your platform to become a burden.

I've discovered that cultivating gratitude for what we have undermines the power of envy. So focus more on *using* your platform for actual good than *growing* it for potential good. Rejoice in whatever influence you've been given, however small. Be grateful for it. Cultivate it like a precious garden in a desert.

It's also healthy and freeing to regularly offer our influence back to the Lord. Lay it down before him and seek to be genuinely okay with him taking it away, if only you can have more of him.

Make Extra Efforts at Kindness

I've often thought that social media is one of our culture's mechanisms for public shaming. What we used to do by locking people in stocks in the village square we now do with "ratioing" and "canceling."

The scary thing is that people who engage in this kind of activity often get more attention as a result. It's a sobering indication of human sin that in certain contexts we not only tolerate meanness and outrage, but we actually reward them.

In light of the state of our cultural dialogue and the nature of the medium, we must work all the harder to display kindness. Take extra steps to say something positive whenever you can. Avoid sarcasm more than you normally would. Be extra eager for opportunities to honor someone else (Rom. 12:10).

I know this isn't simple, and I don't want to take away from the value of open disagreement and debate. And certainly, there is a time for rebuke and indignation. Some attacks or misrepresentations require a forceful response.

Still, it's worth asking with any tweet or post: Does this feel as if it's coming more from the flesh or the Spirit? What culture am I contributing to?

Take Breaks

I am convinced that regular disengagement is essential to healthy usage of social media. In addition to taking sabbath breaks away from social media altogether, you might also consider:

- Delete the social-media apps on your phone—just use it on your computer (either do this always or for certain seasons, such as weekends or family days).
- Have certain places in your home where you never bring your devices (e.g., a den or study).
- Use the "Do not disturb" function as a default practice so your phone stops buzzing at you—the constant distraction is not healthy for us.

Another helpful practice is, quite simply, to mute or unfollow people who consistently drag you down. Don't hesitate to do this. You're not required to follow anyone (or interact with any comments) when doing so is detrimental to your soul. When I'm struggling with envy or loneliness while scrolling through social media, I know it's probably time to disengage for a while.

If you never argue with people in real life, but you do on Facebook, it's time to balance the two out more. Social media should complement, not compensate for, face-to-face interaction.

Final Appeal

Those of us who go by the name of Christ must be especially mindful of how we talk to one another. Our interactions on social media play out before a watching world. Even amid our disagreements, we should be distinguished by love (John 13:35), lest we discredit the gospel.

I realize there are some people with whom it is next to impossible to have an edifying interaction. Truly, I think we often need to give greater thought to Titus 3:10 in such instances: "As for a person who stirs up division, after warning him once and then twice, have nothing more to do with him." It might sound harsh, but wisdom sometimes requires total avoidance. Paul understood this, and so should we.

So much is out of our control. We cannot stop the incessant screaming and scrambling that is the internet. But we can try to reduce our own involvement in the problems and do whatever we can to contribute to a healthier culture. Here's a happy goal to pray for: that more Christians would be recognizable on social media by the wisdom that James describes as "peaceable, gentle, open to reason, full of mercy and good fruits, impartial and sincere" (James 3:17).

In everything we do on social media, Spurgeon's advice gives us a wonderful target to aim for: *say much of what the Lord has done for you, but say little of what you have done for the Lord.*

And here is a wonderful strategy: to fill our hearts so full of the gospel that this is what we *want* to do. How happy is this thought: to be so captivated by Christ's love that we'd *rather* talk about him than ourselves. Truly, there is joy in that place.

Lord, forgive us where we have misused social media. Fill the deepest places in our souls with your love so that we overflow with love and joy toward others in all we do and say.

General Index

Scripture Index

Union

We fuel reformation in churches and lives.

Union Publishing invests in the next generation of leaders with theology that gives them a taste for a deeper knowledge of God. From books to our free online content, we are committed to producing excellent resources that will refresh, transform, and grow believers and their churches.

We want people everywhere to know, love, and enjoy God, glorifying him in everything they do. For this reason, we've collected hundreds of free articles, podcasts, book chapters, and video content for our free online collection. We also produce a fresh stream of written, audio, and video resources to help you to be more fully alive in the truth, goodness, and beauty of Jesus.

If you are hungry for reformational resources that will help you delight in God and grow in Christ, we'd love for you to visit us at unionpublishing.org.

unionpublishing.org